*EASY SPORTS READERS*

# WHAT IS YOUR GAME?
# BASKETBALL

**authors:** Jeri Burton and Tonya Cogan
**illustrations:** Sherry Hermreck and Larry Bauer
**art director:** Elayne Roberts
**imaging:** Larry Bauer

## Word List

| | | | |
|---|---|---|---|
| I | name | what | reporter |
| basketball | you | in | play |
| game | your | on | am |
| court | shoot | like | a |
| two | ball | the | do |
| score | is | pass | with |
| points | this | dribble | |
| team | my | net | |

## Teacher Created Materials, Inc.

P.O. Box 1040
HUNTINGTON BEACH, CA 92647
© 1996 Teacher Created Materials, Inc.
ISBN 1-55734-893-6

# EASY SPORTS READERS

# BASKETBALL

# WHAT IS YOUR GAME?

Teacher
Created
Materials

**Teacher Created Materials, Inc.**

TCM 893

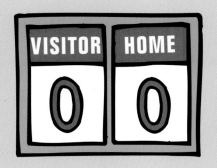

8

VISITOR HOME
0 2

11

# Do you like basketball?